Small Acts of Kindness

five one-act plays

Sherry Kramer

BROADWAY PLAY PUBLISHING INC
224 E 62nd St, NY, NY 10065
www.broadwayplaypub.com
info@broadwayplaypub.com

Small Acts Of Kindness
© Copyright 2016 by Sherry Kramer

All rights reserved. This work is fully protected under the copyright laws of the United States of America. No part of this publication may be photocopied, reproduced, stored in a retrieval system, or transmitted, in any form or by any means, electronic, mechanical, recording, or otherwise, without the prior permission of the publisher. Additional copies of this play are available from the publisher.

Written permission is required for live performance of any sort. This includes readings, cuttings, scenes, and excerpts. For amateur and stock performances, please contact Broadway Play Publishing Inc. For all other rights the author c/o B P P I.

HOLD FOR THREE was first published by B P P I in the collection *Short Pieces From New Dramatists*. THE WORLD AT ABSOLUTE ZERO was first published by B P P I with WHAT A MAN WEIGHS.

First printing: December 2016
I S B N: 978-0-88145-550-2

Book design: Marie Donovan
Page make-up: Adobe InDesign
Typeface: Palatino
Printed and bound in the U S A

CONTENTS

CAKE

The original production of CAKE was at the Source Theatre Festival (CulturalDC, Producer) in Washington, DC in June 2013. The cast and creative contributors were:

PACO ....Chris Aldrich
SCOTT .... Frank Turner
LILY .... Amie Cazel
SAMSARA .... Mia Branco

Director ....Maureen Monterubio
Costumes, props ....Joni Martin
Sound .... Elisheba Itoop
Light ....Sean Forsythe
Production stage manager ....Patrick Magill

CHARACTERS

PACO, *a long hair Chihuahua*

SAMSARA, *a long hair Chihuahua/miniature Italian greyhound mix*

LILY, *a woman in her late 40s*

SCOTT, *a man in his late 40s*

Setting: The second floor porch of LILY and SCOTT's house. It's twilight. The light is soft and magical, and slightly dramatic. The sound of crickets—a perfect summer evening.

(SCOTT *is sitting in an oversized rattan chair with his feet up on a matching, huge comfy rattan ottoman.* PACO *is sitting on the ottoman at his feet.* LILY *is standing.* PACO *often speaks to the audience.*)

PACO: Hello. My name is Paco. And I was made for love.

SCOTT: They're my dogs, I can give them to who ever I want.

PACO: Of all the dogs in the world, only one breed was bred for love.

LILY: What are you talking about, they're my dogs too.

PACO: The Chihuahua.

SCOTT: Nope. I brought them to the marriage, so they're mine.

(SAMSARA, *half Chihuahua, half miniature Italian Greyhound, all trouble, walks onto the porch. She is gorgeous and she knows it.*)

PACO: It is true that Samsara is only half Chihuahua— her father was a dyspeptic miniature Italian greyhound named Peppi—that's who she got her long, exquisite legs and her short temper from, but still. The breeding for love is deeply etched in her blood and bones.

SAMSARA: And there isn't a damn thing I can do about it.

PACO: Darling—don't talk like that.

(SAMSARA *walks past* PACO *and preens for a bit.*)

SAMSARA: I'd rather be made for retrieving. Or sheep herding.

PACO: You hate sheep.

SAMSARA: So? That would probably make me better at it. All I'm saying is—I wish I'd been breed for something productive. Something honest. Something I could be proud of doing, at the end of the day. What do *I* do? I smell the smell of love twenty-four/seven. And when I am not busy *smelling* love, I smell *like* love. That's something to be proud of? I wish I'd been bred for anything other than love. *(She walks around the ottoman and back into the house.)*

(PACO looks at SAMSARA's long legs with admiration. He sighs.)

PACO: Being bred for love is less convenient than you might expect.

SCOTT: I'm giving them to my sister. You won't sacrifice enough for them.

LILY: I don't need to sacrifice anything for them, Scott. I love them! When you love someone you don't have to measure what you gave up.

PACO: How is it inconvenient, you ask? Let me count the ways.

LILY: You don't have to measure how much it hurts to prove you love someone!

PACO: First, there is no ultimate measure of love. And then there is the way love smells. Which—surprise? Is not always so sweet. *(Sniffs loudly)* Smell that? Love, when you measure it, stInks. But I have no choice.

LILY: You know I love them as much as you do.

PACO: If love is anywhere, no matter how badly it smells, I must smell it. *(Puts his paws over his nose to try to keep from smelling)*

LILY: I might even love them more.

(The smell almost overpowers PACO. *He pinches his nose tightly and bravely goes on.)*

PACO: Does she or doesn't she love us more, you ask? *(Shrugs)* It's a stupid question. There is no more or less, no as much or as not. It either smells like love, or it doesn't.

LILY: And unlike you, I love them all the time!

SCOTT: I love Paco all the time.

LILY: No you don't, you love him maybe eighty-seven percent of the time.

PACO: *(He lets go of his nose.)* Sacrilege! Outrage! Not true! His love for me is eternal, like the stars!

LILY: On a good day, you love him, but when he's bad? When he pees on the oriental?

SAMSARA: *(O S)* Paco! Not again! Not the oriental.

SCOTT: That's different. That carpet was my grandmother's.

SAMSARA: *(O S)* Paco, you promised!

PACO: You know I can't help it! The oriental is lush and dark and unless they catch me at it they can't tell for sure—but he still loves me when I pee on it! Even when he catches me he loves me! I can smell it! I can always smell love.

SAMSARA: *(She walks onto the porch and gets up on the ottoman with* PACO.*)* And they can smell when you pee on the oriental.

PACO: No, they can't! I have proven that time and time again.

SAMSARA: They try to smell it. They walk on it barefoot to check for wet spots, they crawl on their hands and knees sniffing—

PACO: But the oriental is a true friend. It absorbs everything like a sponge. After all, it's not as if I am a great Dane. I am a Chihuahua—we are talking a delicate rain, not a monsoon. And as for the smell— well, I have a theory—it is something I have given much thought to. It is my theory that they don't smell it because my pee smells like love!

SAMSARA: You have got to be kidding me.

PACO: But how else can you explain it!

SAMSARA: The degree of self delusion here—

PACO: You never give my theories a chance! You just shoot them down! You never once—

SAMSARA: Please!!!! You're just lucky they love you so much. No matter how strong the smell of your pee, their love for you smells stronger. It blocks the pee-smell out.

PACO: That is the conventional wisdom when it comes to peeing in the house. But in my opinion—

SAMSARA: It's the conventional wisdom because in house after house, with ruined carpets and stinking couch legs, all over the world, it has been proven to be the truth. If it weren't true, a thousand dogs would be put in gunny sacks and drowned every day! Those houses reek! But love is stronger. And don't get me started on cats and their owners.

PACO: You reject the possibility that my pee smells like love.

SAMSARA: Your pee smells like pee. Their love is stronger. End of discussion.

SCOTT: Don't you get tired of him peeing on the oriental all the time?

LILY: Tired, yes.

SCOTT: See!

LILY: Tired is not the same as not loving.

SAMSARA: Don't you ever get tired of it? Of smelling all their love?

PACO: We were made for one thing only—to attach to them and never to be unattached! Stop asking me to betray my D N A!

SCOTT: It's not a crime to hate him when he pees on the oriental! Who wouldn't.

LILY: I don't.

PACO: I will never tire of smelling it! I will never tire of smelling love!

SCOTT: Well, that's because it's not your grandmother's priceless rug.

LILY: I'm the one who has to clean it up, aren't I? And I still don't hate him.

SCOTT: Then why do you hate me?

LILY: I don't hate you.

SCOTT: You do, you hate me. You hate me every time you have to clean up after me. Don't deny it.

LILY: Sweetheart, you're upset about this morning, well don't be, I didn't even notice that—

SCOTT: I'm not talking about that, I'm talking about cleaning up things like—the thing with the I R S.

LILY: Oh. Well, that was hard. When they seized the business for back taxes.

SCOTT: The three times I let my health insurance lapse and didn't tell you.

(SAMSARA *puts her paw over* PACO's *nose, and he puts his paw over hers.*)

LILY: Oh, God, Scott, don't remind me about that. That was bad. Really bad.

PACO: *(But he and* SAMSARA *are in agony from the smells.)*
Hold your breath, my darling, these things never last
long.

*(*PACO *and* SAMSARA *hold their breath.)*

SCOTT: The stock tip I gave your mother that—

LILY: Scott, please. My mother—is fine. She didn't need
that big house. It really was too much for her. I didn't
hate you for any of those things. The only time I hated
you—

SCOTT: Ah ha! I knew you hated me!

LILY: —was the time with the cake.

PACO: *(Gasping for air)* Oh, no, not the cake. Why does
she bring up the cake! *(He tries to stuff tissue, anything
into his nose to keep from smelling it.)* I can't stand the
smell of that cake story.

SCOTT: I'm sorry about the cake, Lily. I don't know
why I did that.

SAMSARA: Oh, no, Paco. Not this time. This time, it's
time to grow up.

*(*PACO *and* SAMSARA *struggle, but she removes whatever he
has managed to stuff up his nose.)*

SAMSARA: This is a man you love, who you insist on
loving, whose love for you *you* are happy to smell!
You must take the bitter with the sweet! You insist
on loving him, on smelling his love—so wake up
and smell the cake story, buster. Even though, in my
opinion, it is not possible to love a man who has done a
thing like this!

PACO: That is the greyhound in you talking! A full
blooded Chihuahua would know! I *must* love him! It is
not possible to do anything else.

LILY: Valentines Day. You told me to go pick it up at
the bakery. You said you'd ordered it special to say

"LILY, I LOVE YOU MORE THAN LIFE ITSELF". And
then when I got it home and opened the box—

SCOTT: I'm sorry! I've said I'm sorry. You know I'm
sorry.

LILY: It said nothing. Nothing at all. It was a blank
cake. And you let me call the bakery and scream at
them, you stood there and listened to me scream at
the counter girl and then you listened to me pry the
owner's number out of her and call him and scream at
him. Because my cake did not say "Lily, I love you",
my cake said nothing, and my last Valentines Day had
been ruined and by God I was going to make sure that
somebody paid! But you'd never ordered it. You'd
ordered a plain cake and told me to pick it up. You
ordered a cake that did not say I love you and then you
told me that it did.

I hated you for that. And I still do.

(PACO *goes over to* SCOTT, *and licks his cheek.*)

LILY: Oh, Paco, how could he do that?

SAMSARA: Yes, I want to that know too. How could he!

PACO: I don't know. It is not in my blood to know. But
the sorrow I feel for him that he *can* do such a thing?

(PACO *licks* SCOTT's *other cheek,* SCOTT *holds him.*)

PACO: Makes me love him even more.

SAMSARA: Oh, Paco. And that's why *I* love *you.*

(SAMSARA *goes over to* PACO, *and nuzzles him.*)

PACO: You see, Samsara? You don't want to love me
for it, but you have no choice. Love. It is hardwired in
us both.

SAMSARA: Then why can't he say it? If he loves her—
and I admit it, Paco, I can smell it too, he does love her!
So why can't he say I love you to her? Why can't he put
it on a cake?

PACO: He tried. He tried so hard. He was on the phone to the girl at the bakery and she asked him if he wanted the cake to say something. One minute the words I LOVE YOU LILY MORE THAN LIFE ITSELF were coming out of his mouth. And the next moment—the thought of putting them on a cake made him afraid. And the moment after that he knew that either the cake would say that, or nothing. He could say nothing less. So he said nothing at all.
But Samsara, in the end the cake *did* say I love you more than life itself.

SAMSARA: No, it didn't—

PACO: It did. Just not in words. I could smell it then. You can smell it now. He loves her more than life itself.

SCOTT: Lily?

LILY: Yes.

SCOTT: Of course you get the dogs. You think I'd give them to my sister? The first time Paco peed on her bed, she'd have him put down. She'd make Samsara wear little doggie dresses. No way is she getting the dogs.

(LILY *goes to them, they all hold each other. A little buzzer goes off.)*

(LILY *kisses* SCOTT, *then gets a pill box, hands him some pills and a glass of water.)*

(PACO *and* SAMSARA *carefully watch him take his pills. There are lots of them.)*

SAMSARA: How long?

PACO: *(Sniffs the air carefully)* A week or two. Maybe three.

SAMSARA: You're sure? When I try to smell it— *(She sniffs.)* It seems a hundred years away. It smells— *(She sniff again.)* As if he isn't sick at all. *(She sniffs.)* It smells—

PACO: You're downwind of her, darling, that's all. The smell of her love is stronger than the truth.

SAMSARA: *(She moves around so she is on* SCOTT's *other side. Sniffs. Sadly.)* Oh. Yes. You're right. *(She leans tenderly into* SCOTT's *side.)* I admit it, Paco. I act like I'm tired of it, like I don't need it, but the truth is I'll miss it.

PACO: When he isn't here to love us?

SAMSARA: No, when he isn't here for *us* to love *him*.

PACO: Ah. Yes. That is the hardest thing, I know.

SAMSARA: When he dies, where will the smell of all our love for him go?

PACO: Didn't your mother teach you this?

SAMSARA: No, I looked too much like my father, and she held it against me.

PACO: My darling. It is the one convenient thing about being bred for love. The smell of love doesn't go anywhere.

*(*SCOTT *finishes taking his pills. The two dogs,* LILY *and* SCOTT *take deep breaths, inhaling as if trying to take in the scent of the entire world.)*

PACO: It never goes away.

(Blackout)

END OF PLAY

HOLD FOR THREE

CHARACTERS

SCOTTIE, *a young woman, late teens or very early 20s*
BARTEY, *a young woman, late teens or very early 20s*
ED, *a young man, late teens or very early 20s*

(BARTEY, ED *and* SCOTTIE *are at the beach, at the water's edge. The horizon exists on a line parallel with the top of the audience.)*

SCOTTIE: *(She is pointing at the moon, which has just started to rise.)* She's up—she's up. ED!! *(She grabs* ED *by the shoulders.)* This is it, Ed. You can do it! Take a big one!

*(*ED *takes in a huge breath of air.* SCOTTIE *yells at* BARTEY.)*

SCOTTIE: Time!

BARTEY: This is ridiculous—he's not going to be able to hold his breath while the moon comes up—

SCOTTIE: Come on, come on, look at your watch—

BARTEY: Okay, okay. It is exactly— *(She looks at her watch, and reports whatever time it actually is.)* _____ and seventeen seconds.

SCOTTIE: Let's subtract five seconds to adjust for operator error, shall we?

BARTEY: What do I care, Scottie? Really…

SCOTTIE: Okay, now, Ed, the first thirty seconds or so are easy. Just relax and save yourself.

BARTEY: *(Looking at* ED, *shaking her head)* You're weird.

SCOTTIE: Adjusted time from start?

BARTEY: Uh—twenty-three seconds.

SCOTTIE: Okay. Alllllllllright.

(Coaching sequences are down directly to ED, *as excited as possible.)*

SCOTTIE: Now. I want you to imagine that you are in mega star 3D disaster film with Bruce Willis, Brad Pitt, and Angelina Joli. You are underwater in—in a nuclear submarine. Angelina is trapped in the compartment where ballistic missiles are armed and ready to fly. You got to hold your breath long enough to get in, rescue her, disarm six missiles, and save the world from nuclear holocaust. Got that?

*(*ED *nods, and mimes spinning open bulkheads, disarming missiles, etc.)*

SCOTTIE: Well. That ought to take him a while. Time?

BARTEY: He's never going to make it.

SCOTTIE: Give me a break. It's almost a third of the way up.

BARTEY: A third? A third? His eyebrows just popped up—

SCOTTIE: The man in the moon does not have—

BARTEY: Well, if he did, that's what we'd—oooh—here come the eyes—

SCOTTIE: Time, damn it, time—I got a man here trying to do a job—

BARTEY: Fifty three seconds.

SCOTTIE: Okay. Here we go. *(To* ED*)* You're Ann Frank. Three storm troopers with boots polished to a shine hard enough to bounce laser beams enter the room. You're hiding in a pile of dirty laundry. One breath out of you—you'll feel the cold steel of their bayonets.

*(*ED *crouches on the floor, his hands covering his head, keeping very, very still.)*

SCOTTIE: Not bad, huh?

(ED *makes a mezzo, mezzo gesture with one hand.*)

BARTEY: *(Looking closely at* ED*)* He's turning blue.

SCOTTIE: *(Looks carefully, too)* He just didn't shave this morning, that's all.

BARTEY: And he's shaking, I think—

SCOTTIE: *(Looking at the moon)* It's close to halfway, wouldn't you say?

BARTEY: Why is he shaking like that—

SCOTTIE: Oh, differences in temperature in the atmospheric layers, something like that I guess. Distorts the air waves.

BARTEY: No, not the moon. Ed.

SCOTTIE: So he's shaking a little. Look—the bridge is up!

BARTEY: What?

SCOTTIE: Of his nose. Bridge is up, get it?

BARTEY: I hope he doesn't pass out or anything—I mean what if he hyperventilates in reverse or something—what if he forgets how to breathe—

SCOTTIE: *(As Carl Sagan)* It took the genetic ancestors of Ed Carmichael billions and billions of years to learn to use their lungs. *(As herself)* Even Ed can't screw all that up in three minutes. Time!

BARTEY: One minute, thirty-eight seconds.

SCOTTIE: And the boy is sweating bullets. I know you're gonna love this one, Ed.
It's 1969. You're president of your university's S D S. The anti-war protest seems to be coming along fine when—TEAR GAS!!!! The pigs have just lobbed in the tear gas—one whiff and you're reduced to a slobbering flower child—you've got to hold your breath long enough to take over the dean's office—GO FOR IT!!!!!

(ED *mimes running, choking on tear gas, fighting with policemen, etc.*)

SCOTTIE: Time?

BARTEY: One minute, fifty-eight.

SCOTTIE: (*Looking at the moon*) Looks like we're getting into the mouth now. Ed—Ed, hang on, just a couple lips to go.

(ED *indicates that he just can't go on.*)

SCOTTIE: Ed—Ed—don't give up now—come on, come on, you can do it—all you have to do is pretend you're—pretend you're—GOD!!! Yes, you're God, and it's Day One of Creation. You've got a whole world of things to make before you get around to breathing the breath of life into Adam, so you hold it—you hold your breath for five days of creatures and firmament and shrubs—only you can do it, Ed, because you're GOD!

(ED *is past making a rude response to this one. He struggles on.*)

(SCOTTIE *is near hysteria.*)

SCOTTIE: TIME!!!

BARTEY: Two minutes, twenty-three.

SCOTTIE: THE HOME STRETCH!!! We're getting into the chin, now. You'll never *guess* what I've saved for the home stretch.

(ED *struggles to his feet and stands, ready.*)

SCOTTIE: You've been unjustly convicted of murder, and sentenced to the gas chamber. You're strapped in—when NEW EVIDENCE PROMPTS A PARDON FROM THE GOVERNOR—but—THE GAS PELLETS HAVE ALREADY BEEN RELEASED!!!!!! The guards are rushing to the door to save you—if only you can hold your breath till—

(ED *pretends sitting in the chair, ripping off the restraining straps, going wild trying to hold his breath in the gas chamber.*)

SCOTTIE: TIME!!!

BARTEY: Two minutes, firty-four—

SCOTTIE: They're rushing to save you—

BARTEY: Clearing the chin now— *(She is now caught up in the excitement.)*

SCOTTIE: They're almost to the door now—

BARTEY: Just this much more to go— *(Makes an eighth of an inch with thumb and first finger, after measuring on the horizon.)*

SCOTTIE: They're at the door—

BARTEY: Two minutes and—you can do it, come on—

SCOTTIE: They're opening the door—

BARTEY: TEN—

SCOTTIE: No, it's stuck—

BARTEY: NINE—

SCOTTIE: They're using brute force—

BARTEY: EIGHT—

SCOTTIE: The guards have asked for help from—

BARTEY: SEVEN—

SCOTTIE: —the people from the press—

BARTEY: SIX—

SCOTTIE: The reporters are throwing their weight around—

BARTEY: FIVE—

SCOTTIE: The door starts to give—

BARTEY: FOUR—

SCOTTIE: It starts to give—

BARTEY: THREE—

SCOTTIE: (*Looking at the moon rather than* ED) Come on, come on, it's starting to give now—

BARTEY: TWO—

SCOTTIE: It's—it's—it's completely UP!!!!

(ED *collapses on the floor.*)

BARTEY: ONE!!!! HE DID IT!!!! THREE MINUTES FLAT!!!

(BARTEY *and* SCOTTIE *gaze at the moon for several seconds.*)

SCOTTIE: Beautiful, isn't it, Ed.

ED: (*Raises his head, looks at the moon for the first time*) Yeah.

(*Beat*)

(*Blackout*)

END OF PLAY

THE DREAM HOUSE

THE DREAM HOUSE was commissioned by The Moscow Art Theatre and the University of Iowa International Writing Program.

CHARACTERS & SETTING

THE WOMAN WHO BUYS THE DREAM HOUSE:

MANDY, *59 years old, permanently broken foot, madly in love with the natural world, believes it loves her back. She might be wrong. She might be right. Any race.*

THE POTENTIALLY ANIMAL SPIRIT GUIDES:

The potentially animal spirit guides should be clowns, and can be played by comedic actors with an expansive understanding of their physical possibilities on stage. They can be any race, and JERRY and THE SKUNK can be any gender.

These characters can be imagined in the Commedia dell'arte tradition, or they can all be puppets, or the Skunk can be commedia influenced but the Snake seems more Alice in Wonderland. If MAURIZIO is a Roku puppet, manipulated by three puppeteers, then maybe the snake is a wooden marionette controlled by someone from a catwalk and THE SKUNK seems to have walked out of a Jim Hansen production. The Spirit Animals do not need to match each other in size, style, or conception.

MAURIZIO, *a giant green frog with a gift*

JERRY, *a three foot garter snake with attitude*

THE SKUNK, *a skunk with an inferiority complex*

THE WOODSMAN WHO BELIEVES IN DANCING
ONE WAY OR THE OTHER:

KEVIN, *a good man. How is he good? Good with trees, for
instance. He may wear flannel. He's a ruggedly handsome
guy who also plays a King in Mandy's dream. Any race.*

THE BRAIN TUMOR WHO IS THE SECRET CENTER
OF IT ALL:

TUMOR, *a sad sack of a character, literally and figuratively.
Young, troubled, ambitious. Any race or gender.*

Setting: A Country Road. A Tree. Evening.

MANDY: *(To the audience)* One day, after years of longing and doing without, I bought a house in the woods that I had always dreamed of. It came with three animal spirit guides.

First, there was a huge frog I called Maurizio. He was the biggest frog anyone had ever seen.

(MAURIZIO swaggers on stage.)

MANDY: His arms and legs, at full extension, were almost two feet long.

(MAURIZIO extends his arms to show his impressive arm span.)

MANDY: He had a prodigious gift—he was able to leap out of my swimming pool even though it's impossible for a four pound frog to do that. A four ounce frog? Sure. They can use the surface tension to escape. But a four pound one? I've talked to scientists. Can't be done. But every day, Maurizio did his laps in the pool, and every day we chased him with the skimmer net trying to catch him so he wouldn't die of chlorine poisoning. Which we couldn't, because he swam faster than we could run. Every night we checked the pool, knowing we would find the body. But we never did. Somehow he always managed to escape.

(JERRY appears.)

MANDY: The second spirit guide who came to me was a snake. I named him Jerry. He was brazen about sunbathing on the stone steps that led to the pool, where his protective coloring made him blend in so perfectly you almost killed yourself not stepping on him. He had no gifts that I knew of.

(A huge white SKUNK *appears.)*

MANDY: And my third spirit animal guide was a skunk. I didn't name him, because you don't name skunks. You do not want them to come when you call. I knew these were my animal spirit guides, who had been sent to protect and watch over me.

MAURIZIO: *(To the audience)* Protect and watch over her? Give me a break. I came to swim in the pool. The water's cool and clean, and it's safe. Other than those idiots chasing me with a net, in that pool I had no natural predators.

JERRY: *(To the audience)* Guide, schmide. I've lived in those rock steps my whole life. People come, people go. As long as they don't step on me, I could care less. I live by the time honored snake motto: I won't tread on you if you don't tread on me.

THE SKUNK: *(To the audience)* Look, I don't know what the hell she's talking about either. She bought a house dead center in my ranging territory. Naturally every night I range on by. Oh, and by the way, Maurizio isn't the only one with a gift. I have one too. When I get scared, I can spray this special attack smell. Let me tell you, the entire animal kingdom knows about that gift. And when I give it, it's a gift that keeps on giving. Oh, yeah. It keeps on giving for days.

MANDY: One night, after getting one of those blinding headaches I'd been having lately, I dreamed that I was dressed by three lovely handmaidens who looked suspiciously like my animal spirit guides. They magically put me in a glorious red dress.

(The three animals cluster around her, hiding her from our view. When they move aside, just a beat later, MANDY is wearing a glorious red ball gown.)

And after I was dressed, I danced with a King.

(The KING emerges. Perhaps he's the King of a South American country? He's tall and dark and Latiny lover looking.)

MANDY: Traditionally, in dreams, women dance with a dashing young Prince, but I was fifty-nine years old, so a dashing middle-aged King was more age appropriate. Also, I have a broken foot that will never heal— *(She lifts the red gown to reveal that she is wearing a huge Aircast boot.)* But, in the dream, even though my foot was still broken, and I was wearing this same boot, it did not interfere with the dancing at all.

(The KING takes her in his arms and they dance to music which the three animal spirit guides provide from instruments that suddenly appear in their hands. The dancing is wonderful and joyful. MANDY dances the way Anna in the King and I did when she was gliding across the mirrored floor with the King of Siam.)

MANDY: See? If I hadn't told you my foot was broken, you would never have known. Watch this.

(MANDY does a fabulous twirl with the help of the KING.)

MANDY: I'll do it again. *(She does. Then continues dancing)* A person with a permanently broken foot can't do this when they're not dreaming. *(More dancing)* For most people, the best part of a dream is saving someone you love from drowning or coming home after being lost for so long or seeing your mother again who is dead and you miss her so terribly. But when you have a broken foot— *(She executes a lovely, graceful, flowing movement.)* It's hard to beat this. *(She dances for another beat.)* Naturally, just when your dream is perfect the perfect part ends.

(The spirit guides stop playing abruptly, the KING *stops dancing, kisses her hand gently, and disappears.)*

MANDY: And you find yourself in a room with three strangers.

(The spirit guides hold masks in front of their faces to become the strangers.)

MANDY: And for some reason, you feel it's a matter of life or death to tell them about the headaches you get, which are the main side effect of the brain tumor that is growing bigger and bigger inside your head. *(To the Strangers)* My head hurts.

MAURIZIO: *(As* STRANGER*)* So?

MANDY: So I have a headache and I need an aspirin. Does anybody have an aspirin?

SKUNK: *(As* STRANGER*)* Nope.

MAURIZIO: *(As* STRANGER*)* Nope.

JERRY: *(As* STRANGER*)* Nope.

MANDY: *(To audience)* You'd think the least a spirit guide could do is have the occasional aspirin when you need it.

MAURIZIO: *(As* STRANGER*)* We're not your spirit guides. This is a dream. And in this part of it, we're strangers.

MANDY: Okay, "strangers", do you have any aspirin?

(The STRANGERS *glower at her.)*

SKUNK: *(As* STRANGER*)* Why would a stranger give you an aspirin?

MANDY: Because I have a headache?

MAURIZIO: *(As* STRANGER*)*You're giving *me* a headache with this headache stuff. Look. I'll be honest. You look fine. Nobody here is even sure you have a tumor.

JERRY: *(As* STRANGER*)* You say you do.

SKUNK: *(As* STRANGER*)* But we're not so sure.

MANDY: Why would I lie?

MAURIZIO: *(As* STRANGER*)* I don't know. Why would you?

MANDY: *(To the audience)* I wasn't lying. I had an M R I and afterward the doctor showed me the tumor on the screen. It was like a globe the size of a ping pong ball, glowing like it was filled with electric milk. *(She holds a small globe that glows, in the palm of her hand.)* If you go outside in the forest when the full moon is rising, and you hold your hand under the moon so it looks like it's sitting in your hand, that's exactly what it looked like. Except it wasn't in the sky, it was in the center of my brain. The doctors said it was probably benign, but one day it would get too big and press too hard on my optic nerve and first I would lose my peripheral vision and stop seeing things to the side, and then I would stop seeing things altogether. So that's when I decided that I should start doing things while I could still see them. Like buying a house in the enchanted forest I had always dreamed of. Like getting married. I was being brave, I was going for it. And still, if I complained even a little bit about the headaches that a globe of electric milk in your head is liable to cause, everyone around me got cranky.

MAURIZIO: *(As* STRANGER*)* Enough with the tumor!

JERRY: *(As* STRANGER*)* Buck up! Show some backbone!

SKUNK: *(As* STRANGER*)* I've had it up to here with the tumor.

MANDY: *(To the audience)* You know how so often in life when things aren't going your way you can't do anything about it? Well, you can in a dream. You can wake up. So that's what I did. After all it was my wedding day. So I woke up.

(The spirit guides remove their masks.)

JERRY: You're awake. That means that this is the part that isn't a dream. You do know that, don't you?

MANDY: Yes. I'm a little scared, that's all.

JERRY: Do you think you're making a mistake?

MANDY: No. But it's still frightening.

SKUNK: You're being brave.

JERRY: You're going for it.

(All the spirit guides start dressing her in a lovely dress.)

MAURIZIO: Just remember: he's not a King. He may be a King in your dreams, but he isn't out here.

SKUNK: I hope you like the dress we picked out for you.

MANDY: Oh, I do, I do. Is it spun by woodland creatures out of native plants woven in the moonlight?

JERRY: No. Jesus, of course not. It's made in China out of fifty percent linen, fifty percent whatever else was handy, in a factory that crushes the body and souls of the workers while destroying their environment and our economy.

MAURIZIO & THE SKUNK: Jerry!

JERRY: Well, she asked!

THE SKUNK: Don't pay attention to him, he's a crank! Oh, you look lovely. The hems a little long. Just don't trip over it with your boot.

(They finish dressing her. She emerges, resplendent.)

MANDY: Thanks, guys. I'm so grateful that you're my animal spirit guides.

MAURIZIO: I'm not your spirit guide. I am a large green frog with a gift—I have a frog kick so HUGE I can leap out of a swimming pool unaided. That's right. I'm living my actual dream. And in a few seasons, I'll be dead, a victim of Judy Barrow's Pomeranian. I'll be a pile of skin under a pile of leaves. Chasing me around your pool to save me when I didn't need saving did not make me a magical part of your life.

JERRY: I'm not your guide either. In a week I'll be hibernating, but this summer, when I was basking in the sun, eating insects and sleeping? The hundred times you almost stepped on me were not evidence of a spiritual connection to me. They were annoying.

THE SKUNK: You never even named me and you don't care about me. Why should I guide you? And where?

JERRY & MAURIZIO: Yeah!

ALL THREE: *(Together)* We were just living our lives!

THE SKUNK: And you were living yours, and you wanted it to be significant that we were living them side by side—

MAURIZIO: You wanted my prodigious leaping-out-of-the-swimming-pool-gift to mean something about *you*—

JERRY: Every time you almost stepped on me, you felt that we had a relationship.

MANDY: But—didn't you feel it too? A little bit?

JERRY: I'm not saying I'm completely indifferent to you—I'm just saying that almost stepping on me—

MAURIZIO: Chasing me with a net—

THE SKUNK: Ignoring me constantly—

JERRY: Does not mean we matter to each other.

MANDY: Then why do I think it does?

ALL THREE: *(Together)* We think it might be your brain tumor.

(MANDY holds the tumor up. It's bigger. Maybe twice its former size. It fills her hand.)

MAURIZIO: Ordinarily, you wouldn't believe in your dreams.

THE SKUNK: Ordinarily, you wouldn't believe that you were connected to everything that crossed your path.

JERRY: Ordinarily, you wouldn't believe in any of this.

MANDY: *(To the audience)* This was not turning out the way I thought it would at all. I thought that if you bought your dream house, if you were brave and going for it, if you believed in your dreams— *(She turns back toward the animals.)* Hey, wait, what if it's my gift to feel these kinds of connections, huh, did you ever think about that, did you? That it's *my* gift? *(To the animals)* Well? What do you have to say?

(MANDY waits for some response from the animals. None)

MANDY: I'm waiting for a response from a snake, a skunk, and a frog. Oh my god, is my brain tumor making me delusional? Wait—that's not the real issue. The real issue is, is my brain tumor making me get married!?

THE SKUNK: Why are you asking us?

JERRY: Do we look like neurosurgeons?

MAURIZIO: If I were you, I'd ask the tumor.

(They all look at the tumor. MANDY puts it in the crook of a branch of the tree. They all circle it, warily.)

MAURIZIO: After all, it grew inside you.

THE SKUNK: Unlike us.

JERRY: Who may have grown to like you a little but when push comes to slither couldn't care less.

(As everyone looks at JERRY.*)*

JERRY: Hey, what do you want from me! I'm an amphibian! That's practically a formal declaration of undying love, for a snake.

MANDY: But can tumors talk?

MAURIZIO: Well, you won't know till you ask it, right?

MANDY: But it's a brain tumor. It can distort or create anything I think it's saying! What if all of this— you, Jerry, the Skunk—what if everything I think is happening is just a tumor induced delusion.

MAURIZIO: Sure, and who knows if the color blue I see is the color blue you see. Enough with the metaphysics! All this is real! Deal with it. The way I see it is, you need to marry this guy and you normally never would, so love called the tumor to you because it needed help making you forget how scary marriage is. Or maybe the tumor was there first, and it needed love to help make you forget how scary brain tumors are. But you won't know if you don't ask it. Come on— what do you have to lose?

JERRY: You can always ignore it, if you don't like what it says.

THE SKUNK: That's good advice!

MANDY: Okay. I'll ask it. *(To the* TUMOR*)* Hello? Mister Tumor? Ms Tumor?

*(*MANDY *looks to the animals. They shrug.)*

MANDY: Could you tell me if I'm getting married because love is real, or because love is a brain tumor induced fantasy? And while you're at it, I wondered if you could tell me about my animal spirit guides. They're— *(She tries to speak confidentially to the* TUMOR.*)*

—they're not really acting the way I'd anticipated. Are they really spirit guides or are they just a brain tumor induced fantasy too? *(The* TUMOR *says nothing. To the animals:)* Great. I don't know if it's saying something and I just can't hear it, or it's saying something and I am too deluded to understand it, or maybe I'm still asleep and this is all just a dream.

ALL THREE: No. This is the part that's not a dream.

MAURIZIO: The dream part was good, but you're awake now. That's the thing about finding out you have a brain tumor. Or any major disease, actually. It wakes you up.

JERRY: So this is the part where you're wide awake.

THE SKUNK: You're almost dressed.

MAURIZIO: And it's your wedding day.

(Different musical instruments appear in the animals' hands. They start playing the wedding march.)

MANDY: *(She takes a step away from them.)* But what if all the love I feel for Kevin and the love I feel he feels for me is a delusion. What if Kevin isn't real?

MAURIZIO: Oh, this guy's real. He grabbed me and threw me out of the pool one time to— *(Air quotes)* —"save me", remember? Almost ripped off my leg.

THE SKUNK: He's so real he has a name—unlike some of us.

MANDY: I don't mean real like that. I know Kevin exists. He walks the earth, he wears a flannel shirt, he's a Lakers fan. I mean what if I believe that he feels some special connection to me the way I believe that *you* feel some special connection to me. What if I'm deluded about him loving me the same way I'm deluded about you guys being my spirit guides?

THE SKUNK: Oh no. Oh my. Oh my God. This is terrible. *(Starts stamping its feet, hyperventilating)*

JERRY: No it's not, it's just cold feet, every bride gets them.

MAURIZIO: Cold feet—we amphibians know all about that.

THE SKUNK: *(Continuing to stamp its feet)* I need some air. Somebody get me a cool compress. Somebody sing Edelweiss to me and hold my hand.

MANDY: What's wrong?

THE SKUNK: SOMEBODY!!! HELP ME!! I'm UPSET! I'm FRIGHTENED! I'm LOSING CONTROL!

MAURIZIO: You're kidding me, right?

THE SKUNK: It's not my fault!

JERRY: Is he going to do what I think he's going to do?

MAURIZIO: You got it.

MANDY: What's going on?

THE SKUNK: IT'S NOT MY FAULT!!!

JERRY: Oh, please! Take some responsibility for your actions!

THE SKUNK: I can't! It's beyond my control. My defense mechanisms are coming on line, engaging my autonomous nervous system. Fear chemicals are racing though my body. They are preparing me to give my gift!

MANDY: What? You mean—

ALL THREE: YES!

(MANDY and JERRY and MAURIZIO take a step back from THE SKUNK.)

MANDY: But why? There's nothing frightening here!

THE SKUNK: You said—what if your love for Kevin and his love for you isn't real! That's the scariest thing I ever heard. In fact, it's so scary that—whoops, I think I just passed the point of no return—everyone, get back, back! —when I'm terrified my instincts take over, I can't help it, I'm going to spray—

(MANDY and MAURIZIO *all run off stage.* JERRY *slithers off stage as fast as he can.*)

JERRY: What a crock! I know if you really tried you could control yourself!

THE SKUNK: I can't! It's my nature! If true love isn't true—who wouldn't spray!

(*Just the* TUMOR *and* THE SKUNK *are alone on stage.* THE SKUNK *quivers and shakes and cries out to the heavens.*)

THE SKUNK: Why is there no one guide me, to help me? No one I can cry out to for help! Why don't I have an animal spirit guide to call on in moments like these! Why? Why? Why?

(THE SKUNK *slowly stops stamping its feet, sobs, sobs, sobs, and falls to the ground, weeping.*)

TUMOR: Okay. So have you got it under control or what?

THE SKUNK: What? Who said that?

TUMOR: Me. Over here.

THE SKUNK: You can talk!

TUMOR: Of course I can talk. All tumors are is talk. What's talk but information, you know? Well, that's all tumors are.

THE SKUNK: But if you can talk, why didn't you answer Mandy's question?

TUMOR: Well, I'm working out my role in her life. I don't want to be branded a good tumor or a bad tumor yet—that's not the aspirational brand I'm interested in.

MANDY: *(O S)* Hey. You okay? Are you going to spray or can we come back?

THE SKUNK: Just give me a minute! *(To the* TUMOR*)* Should I be frightened of you?

TUMOR: No. I'm not your tumor, am I?

THE SKUNK: Well, sort of. Depending on your interpretation of the relationship of the animal spirit guide to the guidee. I think what happens to your— guidee—also happens to you. Of course, I'm not absolutely sure I am her spirit guide in the first place. But I might be.

TUMOR: I see. Well. No. Don't be frightened of me. It's true, I'm getting bigger. But that's my nature. And don't be frightened about love or not love, either. What would be the point? If love could keep you from getting, say, hit by a bus one day on your way to work, or in Maurizio's case, getting eaten by a Pomeranian, then yes, love or not love would be something to be frightened about. But love can't do either of those things. It's just love.
Okay?

THE SKUNK: Okay.

TUMOR: And Kevin's a good guy. Really. Better now?

THE SKUNK: Yes, thank you. I am.

TUMOR: Good. So. Do me a favor? A little one?

THE SKUNK: Sure, if I can.

TUMOR: Higher? Hang me up, a little higher? So I can see everything that's happening on earth?

THE SKUNK: I don't think there's any way to get that high.

TUMOR: I know, I know, but it's this dream I have.

(THE SKUNK *puts the* TUMOR *a little higher on the tree trunk.*)

TUMOR: Tell me, as long as we're talking, do you like being a spirit guide?

THE SKUNK: I'm not sure I am one.

TUMOR: Yeah, I got that. But you might be. So—what's it like?

THE SKUNK: I myself don't like it. Would you? Being part of someone else's dream, when they're not part of yours?

TUMOR: Huh. I hadn't thought of it like that. But don't you get a warm glow from being a spirit guide, a sense of purpose, a sense of connection? All my life, I've had this feeling. I wasn't like other tumors. Everyone said, you'll grow up, you'll figure it out, but the feeling just keeps growing. Of course, that's my nature. But still. I want to be a spirit guide. No, not want to be. Feel that I am.

THE SKUNK: (*Crashes to the ground. It gives up.*) Sorry. That's as high as I can reach.

TUMOR: Could you get some help, maybe?

THE SKUNK: Uhh. Sure, why not. Maurizio! Jerry! Can you come back?

MANDY: (*O S*) What about me?

THE SKUNK: Not yet.

(*They come out.*)

THE SKUNK: Guys, the tumor wants to be higher.

TUMOR: Yes, if you wouldn't mind.

MAURIZIO: Oh, so you can talk after all!

TUMOR: Of course I can talk.

MAURIZIO: Then why didn't you talk before?

TUMOR: Look, Mandy's waiting, if you're not going to help me—

JERRY: You want to get higher, right?

TUMOR: Yes. It's a dream I've had. Please?

MAURIZIO: What the hell, let's get at it.

(They climb on top of each other to get higher in the tree and juggle the TUMOR *as they try to get it higher.)*

MAURIZIO: So, we were all wondering, did you call love to her, or is it love that does the calling?

THE SKUNK: Yeah, are you making her marry Kevin?

TUMOR: A small pressure here. A touch there. That's all it takes.

JERRY: I knew it! I knew it all along!

TUMOR: I didn't say I did it, I'm just saying that's all it would take.

MAURIZIO: Hey, if you did it, take the credit! Don't be shy!

MANDY: *(O S)* Guys! Has the skunk calmed down or not?

ALL: JUST A MINUTE.

TUMOR: In the old days, before modern magnetic imagery brought the brain to light, nobody knew tumors like me even existed. Back then, there were only choices and luck. Now we know all kinds of things about why people do what they do.

(They almost drop the TUMOR.*)*

TUMOR: Be careful! Please! Anyway. Now we know that the Impressionists painted the way they did because they needed glasses and cataract surgery, and George Bush senior invaded Iraq because of a glandular imbalance. But what does it mean to know these things? So Desert Storm was the result of an over active thyroid gland—knowing that doesn't make the people who died in it less dead. And it doesn't make a Monet less lovely, knowing it was caused by nearsightedness.

JERRY: Wow. I understood almost nothing that you just said, but it sounded really intelligent.

TUMOR: *(Fake modesty)* Well. I am a *brain* tumor.

THE SKUNK: It sounds to me like you've given this spirit guide business a lot of thought.

TUMOR: Thank you. I have done the research. It's not something you want to jump into lightly.

MAURIZIO: All I wanted to jump into was a pool, and look where that got me. Attached like a green Sancho Panza to a lame Donna Quixote. Look, is this high enough? Because it's about as high as a frog, and a skunk, and a snake can get.

TUMOR: Oh. Well, it's not as high as in my dreams, but it's much better. Thank you.

MANDY: *(O S)* GUYS! CAN I COME BACK OR NOT!!!

TUMOR: Oh, we'd better let her come back. And let's keep this little chat just between us, okay?

THE SKUNK: *(He calls off.)* Come back. I'm not frightened anymore. It's okay.

(MANDY *comes back as everyone gets down off the tree.)*

MANDY: Look. I have to face facts. I'm fifty-nine years old. I have three spirit animal guides who hold me in contempt, a house in an enchanted forest, and a tumor in my brain that might be impairing my judgment.

JERRY: We don't hold you in contempt.

MANDY: Oh, good.

MAURIZIO: We don't hold you at all.

(They step back from MANDY.*)*

THE SKUNK: In fact, the exact nature of your life and its choices is unknown to you, as it is to most of us.

MANDY: Excuse me? You suddenly became a philosopher?

MAURIZIO: Look. You've got to stop wanting so much from us. Maybe we're your spirit guides, maybe we aren't. So what? You can't make a life with amphibians.

JERRY: Even other amphibians can't.

MAURIZIO: One frog to a lily pad. We're loners.

THE SKUNK: And skunks? When we're frightened? It's gift time as far as the eye can see. We're impossible to live with. So we live alone too.

MAURIZIO: But *you* shouldn't.

JERRY: You should mate.

THE SKUNK: Go on. Do it.

JERRY: We don't have to be your spirit guides to know—it's time.

ALL THREE: It's time.

MANDY: *(Looking at her watch)* Am I late?

THE SKUNK: No, we mean, metaphorically. It's time.

(The man who played the KING *appears, in a flannel shirt in a spotlight in the distance. He no longer looks so very Latiny Kingy.)*

MANDY: There he is.

*(*MANDY *looks at him. He waves.)*

MANDY: There he is. KEVIN!!! HELLO! We're getting married today.

(MANDY *takes a step toward him, but he stays in the spotlight.*)

MANDY: *(To the audience)*It's happening so suddenly. I mean, there's nothing wrong with that, right? Sometimes it seems that all good things do. But I also seem to remember that bad things tend to happen suddenly too. How can you tell them apart? *(She moves away from the tree and the* TUMOR.*)* I'm trying to be brave, but isn't bravery a learning disorder? Like brave people are just people who didn't learn to run away?

TUMOR: *(To the audience)* I never thought about bravery that way. I always thought bravery was one of the very few uncomplicatedly good things there were.

MANDY: *(Still to the audience)* I mean, I know that bravery is good for the species. You need people who aren't smart enough to run away when trouble comes, to give the smart people a chance to get away in time. So bravery is good for the many, but requires the sacrifice of the individual. What if my animal spirit guides—the many—want me to get married because they think I'll be less work that way? What if they're sacrificing the individual—me—for their own comfort?

TUMOR: *(To audience)* Oh my Lord, what if she's right? What if they're just selfish animal spirit guides?

MANDY: *(To audience)* You think your animal spirit guides will guide you. You just assume they will guide you out of the dark parts of the forest and into the light place, and not the other way around.

TUMOR: *(To the animal spirit guides)* Guys! Level with me. Is this marriage a good choice for her or is it a little too convenient?

JERRY: It's a little late now to worry about that, Mister Small Pressure Here, A Touch There.

TUMOR: I didn't SAY I did it, I just said—

JERRY: Marriage is a serious affair.

TUMOR: I know that! But do *you* know that?

MANDY/TUMOR: I'M SCARED.

MAURIZIO: What do we do? Even her tumor is getting cold feet.

JERRY: She's backing out!

MAURIZIO: She's not going for it!

THE SKUNK: I don't blame her for being scared. I know I'd be spraying every which way if I were her. *(He starts stamping his feet a little.)* Oh no, it looks like I'm going to spray in solidarity with her situation.

MAURIZIO: You've got to learn to control that.

THE SKUNK: Easy for you to say. You've got your great big frog kick to get you out of harm's way when you're in trouble.

MAURIZIO: Hey, so I've got a gift, there's no need to be nasty about it.

THE SKUNK: I'm not being nasty, I'm just pointing out that you can't possibly appreciate my situation and what I can control and what I can't.

MAURIZIO: That's true. *(Pause)* Okay. I'll give my frog kick to you.

THE SKUNK: What? Is that even possible?

MAURIZIO: It's a gift, right? So I can give it. That's what gifts are for.

THE SKUNK: But don't you need it?

MAURIZIO: Well, I'm not going to give you all of it. Just enough so you can make a quick getaway when you find yourself in danger. I'll gift part of it to you.

(Suddenly, JERRY *and* MAURIZIO *pick up* THE SKUNK *so he mirror* MAURIZIO's *actions.)*

MAURIZIO: The frog kick is a symmetrical kick where the feet rise to the bum, and in a whipping action press outwards against the water and then come together in a streamline position with pointed toes.
And then—that's when you glide.
The glide is the best part. The glide part is perfect. Like a dream.

THE SKUNK: *(Doing it)* Front legs, back feet, whipping—

MAURIZIO/THE SKUNK: That's it! That's it! Now Gliiiiiiiiide.

(After JERRY *and* MAURIZIO *glide him across the stage in the air, they put* THE SKUNK *down.* THE SKUNK *doesn't stamp its feet. He's calm.)*

MAURIZIO: Better?

THE SKUNK: Much. Thank you. I feel like I can escape anytime. All right. Back to the business at hand. Getting Mandy married.

TUMOR: Why is this so important to all of you?

ALL THREE: What?

TUMOR: I think you're pushing her into this because you're selfish animal spirit guides who want her to get married for your own selfish animal guide reasons.

(The animal spirit guides look at the TUMOR *with a mixture of contempt and pity.)*

THE SKUNK: And you call yourself a brain tumor?

MAURIZIO: I've met little toe tumors with more compassion and common sense.

JERRY: Forget about the Tumor. Leave this to me. *(To the audience)* Guess what? As it turns out, I DO have a gift! A very special one. All snakes do. If a snake circles a couple seven times—they're married.

(JERRY *begins to make a broad circle around the two of them.*)

TUMOR: Wait! Let's think this through.

MAURIZIO: Don't look a gift snake in the mouth.

TUMOR: But this is a big step. Should she be making it with a snake?

JERRY: Stop whining. Hundreds of human beings every year are married in this fashion, without their knowledge or consent.

KEVIN: *(Calling from across the stage)* Hey! Mandy! We're getting married today!

MANDY: Apparently!

JERRY: Of course, even when there is foreknowledge, sometimes the consequences of these unions can be quite catastrophic.

MANDY/TUMOR: I'm scared.

KEVIN: Don't be! I was married once before! The actual getting married, the wedding part? Doesn't hurt! Of course, after the wedding, that's another story.

JERRY: The ability to marry humans is one of the few ways a snake is able to distinguish himself from the rest of the reptile pack. We take this gift very seriously.

MAURIZIO: Yeah? That's not what I heard. I've heard that some snakes marry people as a practical joke.

TUMOR: Is that true? Do snakes marry people as a joke?

JERRY: Sometimes…yes…but oddly enough those marriages often turn out the best.

TUMOR: And when they don't turn out the best?

JERRY: There are no guarantees! Every true spirit guide knows that.

KEVIN: You know what marriage is like? It's like when you're chopping down a tree next to your driveway, and you're sure it's going to fall just right, you've wedged it just like your father taught you—everything you know about cutting down a tree tells you that tree is going to fall harmlessly, back into the woods, next to the compost heap? And instead, it falls right on your house and all that's left of it are splinters? That's what marriage is like most of the time. But that's okay. You can rebuild it.

MANDY/TUMOR: Oh. That's...that's—charming.

TUMOR: In a really odd way. Yes! I'm charmed.

KEVIN: Well, most things you do well in life are like love, you know? And most things you do well in life take a lot of work. Love is like work. I'm not afraid of work. Hey, I'm a woodsman, you know?

JERRY: (*To the audience*) But my private theory about why we marry humans? That I've never shared with anyone before? (*Stage whisper, as he stops circling to share this with us.*) My theory is that snakes are drawn to join two humans together not because we are *their* spirit guides. But because they are *ours*. Yeah. Mandy is *my* animal spirit guide. And I want her to be happy. And to have her own life. Because she's a part of mine. (*He has made one circle around them, and holds up one finger, indicating the circle count.*) One!

KEVIN: But I'm not worried. I've got a really good feeling about our marriage. I feel like that tree is going to fall next to the compost heap, every time. Also, and don't laugh—I've got the feeling that there's a spirit guide watching over us. And I'm not talking about that snake circling us. Say, does he do that all the time?

MANDY: No, usually he just basks in the sun and glares at me when I almost step on him.

KEVIN: Oh.

MANDY: So do you have animal spirit guides too?

KEVIN: Me? No, but my first wife did. She had a chipmunk named Clint who ate her tulip and dahlia bulbs every winter. One day she accidently dropped a fifty pound sack of mushroom mulch on him. I say accidently, but I have my suspicions. Well, you can't stay married to a woman once you have suspicions like that. So we got divorced.

MANDY: Because of her animal spirit guide?

KEVIN: Well, there might have been a few other unresolved issues in the marriage. But you know what? Now that I am thinking about it, it occurs to me that Clint was MY spirit guide. He was just pretending to be hers. He knew I was never getting out of that marriage alive so he sacrificed himself for my happiness. He set me free.

JERRY: (Has completed another circle) Two!

(Now that KEVIN and MANDY are next to one another, it takes less time for JERRY to make a circle.)

MANDY: I didn't know they did that.

KEVIN: Oh, sure. They're generous that way. What do your spirit guides do for you?

MANDY: Oh, we're still in the beginning stages of the relationships. It's a rocky period, but—we're working though it. I think.

KEVIN: Well, good luck with that. Me? I stick with trees.

(Shadows of the tree play over them, light coming from many sources, they are suddenly in the enchanted forest. JERRY continues to circle them.)

When I'm in the forest, when I can see the trees and touch them and hear them in the wind—I don't know. It means something. I feel—different and special. Bigger. Better. That kind of thing.

(JERRY *holds up three fingers.*)

JERRY: Three.

MANDY: I'm glad that you, and the trees, will be the last things that I see.

KEVIN: That's not for awhile, yet, sweetheart. Maybe never. Maybe that tumor won't get bigger and will never press against anything. Maybe—

(KEVIN *takes the* TUMOR, *which is now bigger, out of tree where the other spirit guides put it, and hangs it in the sky. The* TUMOR *might look like a gorgeous full moon. The* TUMOR *glows beautifully in its higher place.*)

KEVIN: Maybe it just wants to be someplace so that it can see everything, so it can see all the way into the future. And it will be happy there.

TUMOR: Yes! This is just the way I dreamed it! Thank you.

KEVIN: You're welcome. *(Pause)* Wait. Who said that? *(He looks around. Doesn't see anyone. Shrugs)* But even if the tumor does grow, and things happen—well, you know what the vows say—in sickness and health, right?

MANDY: Yes, that's what they say—but frankly, I've always hated that line.

KEVIN: ME TOO!!

MANDY: So let's not say it.

KEVIN: Deal! Let's just mean it, okay?

MANDY: Okay.

JERRY: Four! *(He hurries around and holds up four fingers.)*

KEVIN: You know, some people write their vows.

KEVIN: I always get scared when people start reading their home-made vows. I'm afraid they're going to reveal something intimate and ultimately very embarrassing.

KEVIN: ME TOO!

MANDY: But even without the scary vows, this is a scary thing we're doing. Everybody says we're crazy.

KEVIN: Crazier not to do it.

MANDY: True.

JERRY: *(He holds up five fingers.)* FIVE!

KEVIN: Are we married yet? It's funny, I feel like, half married. Maybe more than half.

MANDY: Me too. But I don't think we are quite yet. What will we do after we're married?

KEVIN: The day we met, you told me what a good dancer you were. After we're married, we'll dance.

MANDY: Oh. Dancing. Right. Kevin, there's something I haven't told you.

KEVIN: No kidding! There's like a million things I haven't told you. That's what marriage is for. The telling. Of all those things. We're going to be completely married soon. Tell me then.

MANDY: Wow. You always say the right thing.

KEVIN: Thanks. You too.

(A beat, while KEVIN *and* MANDY *bask in their love.)*

KEVIN: You know, there is one line of the vows that I like.

MANDY: Which one?

KEVIN: "To have and to hold."

MANDY: That's the one line I like too!

(JERRY *desperately circles fast enough to be able to hold up six fingers.*)

JERRY: SIX!!!

KEVIN & MANDY: To have and to hold.

(*They hold out their hands to each other, and embrace. JERRY, who is very close to them, circles them one last time, and holds up seven fingers.*)

JERRY: SEVEN... (*He collapses.*) You may now kiss the bride.

(*They kiss.*)

MANDY: Now we're married.

(*Suddenly* MAURIZIO *and* THE SKUNK *have instruments in their hands.*)

(JERRY *whips his out too. They start to play music.* KEVIN *and* MANDY *dance.*)

(MANDY *dances terribly with her broken foot. They stop.*)

MANDY: I'm sorry. I feel like I've lead you on.

KEVIN: That's okay. It's even okay if you want to lead. I mean, I can lead sometimes, you can lead sometimes. You know what I mean.

MANDY: No, I meant, I've led you on about my dancing. This is one of the million things I haven't told you.
I can't dance at all.

(KEVIN *steps away from* MANDY. *The music abruptly stops.*)

KEVIN: What?

MANDY: But that's okay, isn't it? I mean, you said we didn't have to tell each other everything.

KEVIN: Yeah, but—you said you could dance. The day we met, you told me what a good dancer you were.

JERRY: Oh no. This doesn't sound good.

THE SKUNK: *(He begins to hyperventilate)* It doesn't sound good at all.

MANDY: Wow. I thought you were always going to say the right thing.

KEVIN: Yeah? Well, maybe that is the right thing for me to say.

THE SKUNK: No nonononono. *(He starts stamping his feet. Hyperventilating)* I'm frightened!

MAURIZIO: Control yourself. Feet together!

(THE SKUNK does each movement along with MAURIZIO.)

MAURIZIO: Feet up to the bum, toes bend out, whipping action—

(THE SKUNK does all these things.)

TUMOR: I knew it was too good to be true.

MAURIZIO: —and now glide. Glide. Glide.

TUMOR: I must be delusional! I've got to fight my way out of here—

MAURIZIO: *(To the TUMOR)* You control yourself too!

TUMOR: I can't control myself, out of control is the very nature of who I am!

THE SKUNK: *(Still gliding)* Glide. Glide. Glide. *(Glides off stage)*

MAURIZIO: You're good?

THE SKUNK: *(O S)* I'm free! My gift is not in control of me, I am in control of my gift! I'm cool. I'm calm. *(He comes back on stage.)* Okay. What can I do to help?

JERRY: I don't know—this is the first couple I've ever married!

TUMOR: What do we do? What do we do?

MAURIZIO: That's the problem—we don't know!

TUMOR: But you're her spirit animal guides! If you don't know, who does!

THE SKUNK: A small touch somewhere, a little pressure over there! You can do it! You can fix things in her brain so she could dance! Or, or, we could grab ahold of her leg—

(THE SKUNK *motions for* MAURIZIO *to help. They both awkwardly grab her leg.*)

THE SKUNK: And move it, so she can dance—

(*They try to move her legs, and she loses her balance and starts to fall.* KEVIN *catches her.*)

MANDY: I'm sorry I lied to you. I was pretending it was true, because I like to pretend that I can dance. But the only time I can dance is in my dreams.

In my dreams I sort of glide and sort of float, and you and I spin around and around. And time stops and goes forward at the same time.

KEVIN: Oh! That sounds great! (*He smiles.*) Can you teach me?

MANDY: Teach you what?

KEVIN: To dance so time stops and goes forward at the same time.

MANDY: No, I can only do that in my dreams.

KEVIN: So?

MANDY: So I can't really dance at all. I was just pretending that I could.

KEVIN: Well, my father, in between telling me how to make trees fall where I want them to, told me that the person we pretend to be is usually the best person we are.

MANDY: But it's not who we are. It's a lie.

KEVIN: No, not necessarily.

MANDY: Yes, necessarily. I can only dance in my dreams.

KEVIN: Not a problem.

MANDY: How can it not be a problem? I told you I could dance—

KEVIN: And you can—

MANDY: No I—

KEVIN: If you can only dance in your dreams, then that's where we'll dance.

(The lights change, the spirit guides make music that can't possibly come from the instruments they are using. The forest tree shadows flicker even more enchantedly. The TUMOR *glows but does not grow.)*

*(*KEVIN *holds out his arms to her.)*

KEVIN: Well?

MANDY: You're sure?

KEVIN: To have and to hold. And to dance.

*(*KEVIN *takes* MANDY *in his arms. They dance. She dances beautifully, and he does too.)*

TUMOR: *(Singing)* One day
After years of longing
I bought a house in the woods
That was made out of dreams.

One day
After years of longing
I fell in love with a man
Who could dance in my dreams.

Shine on
Shine on
Like a moon
Your troubles turned to beauty

In the dream house
Of your heart.

(KEVIN *and* MANDY *dance.*)

(*The three animal spirit guides play.*)

(*The brain* TUMOR *hums.*)

(MAURIZIO *may swim.*)

(*Lights fade.*)

END OF PLAY

THE WORLD AT ABSOLUTE ZERO

CHARACTERS & SETTING

DIDI, *she's about thirty-five. She's attractive. But not too attractive. She has an intensity that drives men wild in a variety of ways—sometimes straight into a sexual frenzy, sometimes right out the door, sometimes to a Preston Sturges retrospective marathon at the local art film house.*

FRED, *he's about forty. He's less attractive than* DIDI *is, in the scheme of things. But not unattractive, by any means. He hasn't decided which kind of wild* DIDI's *intensity is going to drive him to. He's had better days.*

DIDI's *apartment. The kitchen. Through the window we can see and hear that it's raining outside. A refrigerator—one of those old rounded white ones would be pleasant. A kitchen table, a couple chairs.*

A six-pack of Coca-Cola.

(Late, late at night. DIDI *is standing at the kitchen window, watching it rain.* FRED *is standing next to her. He is raising his hand, he is about to touch her, he— No. He isn't going to touch her.)*

DIDI: *(With genuine, good-natured interest)* Fred, are you as unattracted to me as I am to you?

FRED: *(Just as good naturedly)* I think so.

DIDI: Still, there is this...urge... *(She moves around him, circling him.)* This...compulsion. It's like I'm out shopping for shoes, and I see this sweater.

*(*FRED *moves to the refrigerator.* DIDI *looks him over, half-heartedly.)*

DIDI: I don't need it, I can't really use it, it doesn't quite fit, but I have this impulse to buy it anyway because is it on sale.

*(*FRED *takes a can of Coke out of the refrigerator.)*

DIDI: Are those cold enough yet?

FRED: They're okay.

DIDI: There's plenty of ice.

FRED: I like it straight out of the can. *(He holds the can up, so it catches the light.)* We are a soda-driven society, you know. And in the driver's seat, is Coke. You pop the top. *(He does.)* You drain it down. *(He starts to chug it down.)* You feel a little bit better, then fifteen minutes later you go back to feeling hostile again.

DIDI: Oh, I hope you didn't take my saying that about shopping personally.

FRED: Me? Why would I take a comparison of sex
with me to a bad day sorting through remnants, out-
size garments, and designer nightmares at Filene's
Basement personally? However, I hope you don't
mind my saying that if I had been even the slightest bit
attracted to you, I would have been very hurt.
If I had.

DIDI: But you're not.

FRED: No. (*Still drinking his Coke*) I'm sorry.

DIDI: Oh, don't be sorry. (*She sits down at the kitchen
table.*) It's just one of those slow-mo emotional train
wrecks you find yourself living, from time to time.
Who would have thought that neither one of us would
be the slightest bit attracted to the other? God knows it
doesn't take much.

FRED: Look, Didi, it's not like when I left the house this
evening—

DIDI: I know that, Fred—

FRED: I didn't set out, hellbent on being unattracted to
you—

DIDI: Fred, believe me—

FRED: Normally, my libido—

DIDI: You don't have to say another word. I know.

(FRED *starts in on the Coke again.*)

DIDI: Still, you have to admit—it goes against the odds.
I mean, think how hard it would be if we were actually
trying to find two attractive single people who have
everything in common but who, after spending seven
hours together, can't manufacture a single drop of the
most common animal attraction for each other?

FRED: Obviously, it's one for the record books. Ripley's
Believe It Or Not. Fred and Didi's Date of Doom—

they'll put us right under the listings for the two-headed goats.

DIDI: No, they'll put us *above* the listing for the two-headed goats. Fred and Didi's Date of Doom, alphabetically, would go before it.

(FRED *looks at her as he crumples the Coke can.*)

DIDI: Well, maybe it's the weather. Some freak Canadian storm barreling out of the frozen North. Or, maybe it's a once-in-a-millennium planetary alignment, my Pluto in your Vega—not that I believe in that sort of thing. Or maybe—maybe it's happening to everyone! Maybe no one on earth is attracted to anyone else tonight!

FRED: Now there's a comforting thought.

DIDI: When I didn't feel it start to happen at dinner, I got a little anxious, but I kept telling myself, sometimes you don't feel it at dinner.

FRED: Sometimes, the times when you don't feel it at dinner are the best times of all.

DIDI: Right.

FRED: Sometimes, you're with the last person on Earth you think you'll be attracted to, you're totally unaware of it, and then it hits you. I like it like that. When it creeps up on you.

DIDI: Like a slow, steady, fatal fever.

FRED: Of course, I also like it when you see her across a room for the first time and something about her just takes you—

DIDI: Your insides start to boil—

FRED: And you have to have her, you have to do it, you have to press your body up against hers or die!

DIDI: It's so wonderful when it happens like that!
It's like—all of a sudden, you feel you're the focus
of all this energy, and power. Possibly all the power
in the world. You feel like it's flooding through you,
radiating out of you, flowing directly from the center of
the earth, just to you.

FRED: You do?

DIDI: Don't you?

FRED: For me it's just…feeling like sticking it in.

DIDI: And…?

FRED: That's all.
But it's a very, very strong…uh…well…feeling.

(FRED *lunges for the refrigerator, yanks out another Coke,
begins drinking it for all he's worth.*)

DIDI: Fred—if you don't mind my asking…is it the
sugar you're after?

FRED: *(Gulping, he replies as he drinks.)* No.

DIDI: The carbonation?

FRED: No.

DIDI: The caffeine?

FRED: No.

DIDI: The trace of phosphorous and sodium?

FRED: You know about the trace of phosphorous?

DIDI: *(Shrugging)* I read labels. So—is it the
phosphorous?

FRED: No. It's a secret formula, you know. Everybody
knows what goes into a can of Coke, but nobody
knows why it turns into Coke in the can. Nobody
knows why Coke connects people. Why it settles them
down, at the same time the caffeine and sugar are
revving them up. It goes against the laws of nature, for

Coke to do what it can do. You sure you don't want one?

DIDI: I'm sure.

FRED: Because you'd be amazed what a Coke can do for a person, it's restorative, it really is—

DIDI: WELL, MAYBE I DON'T WANT TO BE RESTORED! *(Pause)* I mean, I never liked Coke, okay?

FRED: Okay.

DIDI: I'm sorry, Fred.

FRED: What's there to be sorry about? It's just a can of Coke. It's okay.

DIDI: *(Sighing)* We have to face it—

FRED: I know what you're going to say, but let's not jump the gun here—

DIDI: —it's not coming—

FRED: —so it's seven hours late, so what—

DIDI: —it's not your fault and it's not my fault.

FRED: —there's no law that says the time limit is seven hours, after all—

DIDI: —it's just one of those freak accidents. We have to get up and walk away from it. We have to—

FRED: *(Has drained the last sip of Coke; resolutely slams the can on the table)* —IT COULD STILL BE COMING. Now. I have done my very best to feel it, but if you could—

DIDI: Are you saying I'm not trying to feel it?

FRED: Not exactly, Didi—

DIDI: You have no right to say I'm not trying to feel it!

FRED: Okay, okay. I wouldn't say you weren't trying…a little.

DIDI: Oh, you wouldn't. Do you call "little" the fact that I ate everything on my plate even though I detest Tex-Mex?

FRED: You hate Tex-Mex?

DIDI: And I suppose it was "little" that I laughed at everything you said, including the Ollie and Oley jokes, which are really just thinly disguised Polish jokes, which I find bigoted, stupid, and crude?

FRED: *(Crushed)* The Ollie and Oley jokes are my best material.

DIDI: Or maybe you think it was "little" that I have made constant eye contact with you for seven hours, without once smirking, or giving any indication at all that you have a large piece of salsa-stained lettuce stuck in your teeth?

(FRED removes the piece of lettuce, horrified. He buries his face in his hands.)

FRED: It's not coming, Didi.

DIDI: No. It's not.

FRED: Look, I'd better go. I should have left hours ago, as soon as I realized I wasn't attracted to you.

DIDI: Don't be so hard on yourself, Fred. Just because you're unattracted to someone doesn't mean *they're* not attracted to you. Attraction is like a virus. When absolutely necessary, you can lower your resistance— or your standards—and it's contagious. You can catch it from somebody— *(She snaps her fingers.)* —just like that. For all you knew, I *was* attracted to you, and everything was going to work out fine.

FRED: I was pretty sure you weren't attracted to me.

DIDI: You were? Then why didn't you go home?

FRED: Well, I would have, but it just didn't make sense that you wouldn't be a little bit attracted to me, did it?

(DIDI *says nothing.*)

FRED: Think how small a virus is, it's minute, it's infinitesimal...the evening would have worked out fine if you'd just been attracted to even the smallest thing about me—like my sense of humor, for instance.

(FRED *pauses;* DIDI *says nothing*)

FRED: Or the way my eyes crinkle up when I laugh... *(Grasping at straws, or in this case, his shirt)* Or, or, or... my shirt—

DIDI: Oh, I like your shirt.

FRED: You do?

DIDI: Just not enough. *(Silence)* I'm sure the sex would have been very nice, though, if I had.

FRED: Sex as an impulse purchase?

DIDI: Oh, you're generally thrilled with an impulse purchase. At least till you get it home.

FRED: YOU ARE HOME!!!

DIDI: Well, that's the downside. But on the other hand—I'm not the one who has to go home tonight in the rain. *(She is at the window, looking out.)* Oh, look, someone's making a run for it. Look at him go. He's getting soaked, poor bastard.

(FRED *is at the window, watching the poor wet man's progress.*)

DIDI: He'd be better off walking, don't you think? All you do when you run in the rain is get wet faster.

FRED: Oh, I don't know. *(He moves away from the window, despondently, and sits down.)* You don't know what he's running from. Fight or flight. It's an irresistible impulse—like shopping, Didi. I heard it on N P R. Homo Sapiens have two choices, when they're backed into a corner, when they're in a desperate

situation—say, like this. And if they don't fight, and
they don't take flight—you know what they get?
Cancer.
I'm getting it right now. (*He sinks into the chair, head in hands.*)

DIDI: Fred— (*She goes to him, to comfort him.*) Fred, it's
just a date that didn't work out.

FRED: Right this instant the chemistry of my body is
altering. Vital defense mechanisms are breaking down,
giving up. They will no longer recognize the million
daily poisonous free radicals as the enemies they are—
but will welcome them in to rewrite my molecular
structure with open arms.

DIDI: Look, uh, I had pretty high expectations about
this date too, Fred, but don't you think you're taking it
a bit too far?

FRED: It is always a matter of life and death. Anne
Sexton.

DIDI: If the thunder don't get you, the lightning will.
The Grateful Dead.

FRED: By the deeds of man, the world is made, and
unmade every day. Rabbi Naichman.

DIDI: So is a bed. Didi Watson.

FRED: The wheel of life is—just as a general interest
question, did you put fresh sheets on yours?

DIDI: Yes.

FRED: I did too, in case we went back to my place. I feel
like a schmuck about it now, of course. The old ones
weren't even that dirty.

DIDI: I didn't know guys did that. Fred, that's very
sweet.

FRED: It doesn't feel sweet. It feels pathetic.

DIDI: Well, it is pathetic. In retrospect, that is.

FRED: I can feel it starting again. Failed impulses. Thwarted urges. The duplication of bad memories, flooding from one organ to another. Replicated in cell after cell after cell.

DIDI: Look, Fred. If this sort of everyday tragedy gave you cancer, nobody would live long enough to get it. Only seven or eight people would make it past the age of seventeen. If disappointment killed people—hell, when the Beatles broke up the entire baby boom would have dropped dead.

FRED: That's right, that's right. When in doubt, drag the Beatles into it. Disappointment does kill people. They're just too stupid, anymore, to feel it, that's all.

DIDI: Well—I'm no expert—but after the events of this evening, that sounds like an excellent evolutionary adaptation to me.

FRED: What do you think, that you're immune to this? If attraction is like a virus, unattraction is a super virulent strain. Just wait till it starts eating you up. Then we'll see how calm and cool and detached you are.

DIDI: We don't have to wait, Fred. Because I'll tell you. If I woke up tomorrow morning—alone, in my wasted clean sheets—and found a lump in my breast—it would be much easier accepting that the malignancy was caused by the Beatles breaking up than by not being attracted to you.

FRED: *(Outraged!)* You don't have the right to get cancer from the Beatles breaking up! Only they do. It was their disappointment—their date that didn't work out.

DIDI: Fred, I'm sorry you're not attracted to me. I'm sorry I'm not attracted to you. However, I am not ashamed to say that at this moment I am still sorrier that the Beatles broke up. Seriously, aren't you?

FRED: No.

DIDI: You didn't like the Beatles?

FRED: I loved the Beatles. They changed my life.

DIDI: I wouldn't have.

FRED: That's clear.

DIDI: How long does an affair like the one we might have had usually last? Four months? Five?

FRED: Oh, no. We could have deluded ourselves for six or seven months at least.

DIDI: Fine, six or seven months it is. The loss of six or seven months with me, versus the loss of the Beatles. THE BEATLES!!!! How can you even begin to compare the two? I admit that I've spent a few ridiculous moments this evening, imagining our life together, picking out my wedding dress, watching us spend our golden years together. But that's not realistic, Fred. That is not really in the cards.

All that is really in the cards, what you would have ultimately gotten from me, is this:

A six or seven month relationship, at the end of which you have my list of favorite restaurants to add to yours, as places to take future dates.

The secret place to press down hard on a woman's pelvic bone so she'll really come— *(She grabs his hand and places it on her pelvis for an instant.)* —here, right here, got it? Okay?

An untold amount of senseless grief and aggravation— starting with that shirt.

A hell of a lot of great sex.

Some choice cocktail conversation one-liners and jokes, here, here's one, so you won't go away empty-handed: Question: How do you circumcise a whale? Answer: Send down foreskin divers. And that, Fred, would be about it. That would be what you would have gotten out of a relationship with me. But the Beatles...the Beatles, if they had stayed together, would have given you more than I ever could. Except children, I suppose...if we had let it get that far. Which we obviously couldn't.

FRED: Obviously! Because we would be too busy bickering about the Beatles! You think I don't know why you keep retreating into this Beatles nonsense? Well, I do. The breakup of the Beatles, while tragic, is also understandable to you. Other tragedies in your life are incomprehensible, but this, alone among what you consider your great personal catastrophes, makes sense. This one has a reason you can pin down, and understand. Yoko.

DIDI: *(Oh, how ridiculous)* Linda.

FRED: *(Don't make me laugh)* YOKO.

DIDI: *(I'm getting annoyed.)* LINDA.

FRED: *(I'm getting annoyed.)* YOKO.

DIDI: *(Don't you dare say Yoko to me again!)* LINDA!

FRED: *(Panic envelops him.)* What am I doing here! *(He pulls open the refrigerator, takes out a Coke, and drinks it for all he's worth.)* It all started out so normally tonight. I was positive it was coming! Why can't I feel it! Why, all of a sudden, is tonight the night it's gone!

DIDI: I guess that's the way it happens, in the end. All of a sudden, you realize. It's not coming. It's never coming. You will never feel it again.

FRED: (*Chugging desperately*) No, the weather will change. The planets will realign themselves. The strange powers that are keeping us from feeling it—what am I saying? I don't understand what I'm saying. I don't understand anything anymore, if you want to know the truth. Nothing. I have whole days where not a single thing makes sense. Something good happens, I'm not happy about it because I wonder if it might actually be something bad. And you know something else? Lately, if I had to make a choice between something good that doesn't make sense, and something bad that I can understand—I'll take something bad.

DIDI: You don't really mean that Fred.

FRED: Oh yes I do. I could stand anything. If I could just understand it.

DIDI: Anything, Fred?

FRED: Yes. I can't go on and on with nothing making sense. Every time I turn around there's a knife in my back and I can't figure out how it got there. It's not the pain, Didi. I can take the pain. I could take more of it—I know I could. If I knew the answer. If it just made sense. If I knew what I had to stand.

DIDI: Then the good news is the bad news, Fred. Because all you have to understand is—that not understanding is the thing you have to stand.

FRED: (*Doubling over*) Oh, God.

DIDI: Yes. It has the chill of the inevitable, doesn't it? The gut kick of the "Why didn't I see it before?" Not understanding is the thing you have to stand.

FRED: (*Experiencing the gut-kicking chill in all its glory, he lunges for the refrigerator, yanks out a Coke, even though he hasn't finished the other one.*) This is terrible. This is much worse than I thought. It's been getting harder and harder, every time I meet someone, to go out on a date, to do this, to feel it again, but this is definitely the worst. The worst by far. *(He pops the top.)* I keep telling myself— *(Talking and drinking from both Cokes at the same time, alternating, without realizing he's working two Cokes at once, like a cigarette smoker smoking two cigarettes.)* If you hide it they won't see… You think it's written all over your face, that they'll run from you when they see that you don't understand anything, and that you are empty…and cold…and alone… *(He holds both Cokes up at once and realizes. Terror strikes. He may begin to weep.)* God I wish I'd been attracted to you!

DIDI: Yes. Once you get it into bed, even the pain is comforting, familiar. If we could just have made it into bed, we'd be safe from all this. If we could just have made it into bed, we'd be back in the known world.

FRED: I feel… *(The calm that comes after the worst that can possibly happen happens.)* I feel like I've already been through a very comforting, familiar, destructive relationship with you. I feel like we've done every possible stupid thing we can to fool ourselves, and each other, reopened all the standard wounds, given them a chance to heal, opened them up again, and there is no way to keep it up any longer. It's over. *(Longing and regret overpower him again.)* And we never even got to have the sex!

DIDI: But you did get the pelvic bone trick. More than you've gotten out of most relationships, I'll bet.

FRED: Yes, but I haven't gotten the chance to try it out yet.

DIDI: Are you holding out for the names of the restaurants? Here, I'll write them down for you.

FRED: That's not what I want.

DIDI: Then I don't understand. Why are you still here?

FRED: I want to understand. One thing.

DIDI: *(Silence)* All right. Although normally that would be impossible, Fred, this is your lucky day.

FRED: What do you mean?

DIDI: I mean, I'm not attracted to you, you're not attracted to me, so we will just have to do something… else, won't we? *(She sits down on a chair, pats the chair next to her.)* Sit down. I will help you understand one thing.

FRED: Just like that?

DIDI: Well, you know what the alternative is….

FRED: Cancer.

DIDI: Right. So whenever you're ready, begin.

FRED: *(He takes in a deep breath.)* I'm forty years old, my wife left me, the apartment went with her, I feel ridiculous.

DIDI: *(Pause)* Is that it?

FRED: No, no, I feel ridiculous doing this.

DIDI: Surely *that* can't be hard to understand.

FRED: *(Defiantly)* I'm forty years old, my wife left me, the apartment went with her, my mother just died, I have no income to speak of, and much to my surprise, no sex drive. Thank God they still make Coke. Other than that my life is absolute zero.

DIDI: *(Smiling)* Minus four hundred and fifty-nine degrees. That's absolute zero. It's very cold. It is so cold, in fact, that it does not exist naturally. Scientists, in labs, have to manufacture it, at great trouble and expense. They make cold so cold that there is nowhere in the universe that is colder—except, perhaps, in the cold made by other organisms in other galaxies in their absolute zero labs.

You may have stumbled out of the temperate zone tonight, Fred. And strayed into that first little patch of ice and snow. But when it comes to absolute zero, you're just a beginner. A rank amateur. You don't really know anything about absolute zero, Fred. And trust me. You don't want to know.

FRED: Is this supposed to comfort me?

DIDI: *(Shrugging)* In an odd way, I suppose.

FRED: You and reality don't have much of a relationship, do you?

DIDI: I thought we'd worked through the recrimination stage, Fred. I thought we were on our way to something new. But—here— *(She gets another can of Coke out of the refrigerator.)* Have another one. The last two seem to have worn off.

(FRED doesn't take it.)

DIDI: Come on. Take it. Between you, and what you view as absolute zero, there is only this can of Coke. Whatever you can get from it, I suggest you do.

FRED: You don't know the first thing about what I'm going through. You don't even begin to understand.

DIDI: Maybe I do, and maybe I don't, but I'll tell you one thing—you can't let it feed on you like you're letting it. You can't let it eat you up.

FRED: Then what should I let eat me up?

DIDI: What?

FRED: What should I let eat me up? If the fact that every dream I ever had has turned to shit and I have gotten nothing that I wanted isn't terrible enough to eat me up then what is!

DIDI: Good point.

FRED: Maybe it's right to be eaten up when your
dreams go bad. Maybe it's not human not to be. What
kind of a person would I be if I *didn't* let it eat me up!

DIDI: Another excellent point! Except...you still can't
let it.

I know what you're going through. There's nothing
stronger or truer about you than your dreams, right?
Your dreams are kind of like a dog team, a pack of
magnificent animals that can carry you across the ice
no matter how hard the Siberian Express Winds of
Reality blow—your dreams are your protection against
the cold. But what happens when the temperature
drops really low—when things get bad and keep
getting worse—and your dreams start failing you?
What do you do? You start feeding the weak ones to
the strong ones—you sacrifice them, right? You feed
on them yourself. You tell yourself you really didn't
need those weaker dreams, the dreams that couldn't
stand the ice and wind and cold. That's what you tell
yourself. And one day only the strongest dreams are
left. And there really is a kind of justice when their
hunger overwhelms them, and they turn on you. When
your dreams give up, and devour you. You have to
admit it. Compared to your dreams, you're just a
worm. Here are your dreams—brave, magnificent
animals—and they're harnessed to a worm. One worm
to another, Fred, I have to tell you. Being eaten up feels
like the right thing to do.

FRED: Maybe if we'd just done this yesterday, this
wouldn't be happening. Maybe yesterday, we would
have had just enough left and we'd be in bed right now
and everything would be fine.

DIDI: It's sort of like an O'Henry story, isn't it? I go out,
looking for someone who has the one thing I need—

FRED: —and the person I end up finding is out looking for the exact same thing in me. On the night we both run out of the last thing left us. *(Wailing)* It isn't fair!

DIDI: The only difference between us now is that it's a little colder where I am. But I guess I've dropped the temperature a notch or two for you.
I'm sorry. I should have recognized you. I could have stopped it in time.

FRED: It's not your fault.

DIDI: I still should have known. I've been with the tapped out, the drained before. There was the man—oh, he was lovely, haunted, a young, alcoholic, talentless Edgar Allan Poe. His eyes burned through things, and I burned for him. The first time we made love he collapsed beside me and said, "I feel human again". Not "I love you", not "I need you", not even "Thank you". Just "I feel human again". I should have run like hell but I stayed. I was young. I was warm, and he was cold, and I felt the way the warm feel—that I had more than enough for both of us. I still believed. I let him feed. It takes a human to make what we are into a human again, you see?

FRED: We're vampires now?

DIDI: Vampires.

FRED: I think I'll stick with being a worm, if it's all right with you.

DIDI: That's because a worm doesn't have to take responsibility for its mistakes.

FRED: Oh. And vampires do?

DIDI: Well. At least they can if they want to.

FRED: And do you...want to?

DIDI: Take responsibility for this mistake? Absolutely! *(She extends her hand to him.)* Fred, it has been anything but a pleasure meeting you. In fact, meeting you has, in a way, turned into the end of my life. But—it's just one last, lonely, cold mistake in an otherwise empty arctic landscape. *(She heads over to the door.)*

FRED: *(Not following her to the door)* Vampires don't make mistakes.

DIDI: We did.

FRED: Vampires recognize each other. They can't help but recognize their own kind.

DIDI: Maybe so, but we were looking for signs of life. Warm blood. We were looking for heat!

FRED: So? Maybe what we found was something— better.

DIDI: No. No. No nonononono. I know what you're suggesting—it won't work. It can't work.

FRED: But Didi—

DIDI: NO. I DON'T WANT TO! I go out on the street, and I see them, I can tell that they're the living and I'm not, I can tell I don't belong to that world anymore, but I find someone and they let me taste it, for an hour or two. That's what I need! Not someone who's dying to taste it too!

FRED: I'm not attracted to you, you're not attracted to me, let's do something else. That's what you said. Well, okay.

DIDI: But it won't work, how can it work, we don't have anything we need—

FRED: Seems to me one world is pretty much like another, when you get used to it, Didi. The world at absolute zero probably feels like this one, after a while.

DIDI: It freezes you, after a while. The cold starts in your feet. And moves like hemlock, to your heart. And after a while, you don't notice you haven't had a single human emotion for days. You don't notice that all you are is cold.

FRED: No. You acclimate. You adjust. You adapt.

DIDI: You want me to pretend cold isn't cold—that's it! You want me to pretend—

FRED: No, we don't have to pretend anymore, that's the point! We don't have to trick or trap each other. We know what we are! We don't have to go out looking for people to hide things from. Don't you understand, Didi? We're going to be fine now. We're going to be fine.

(FRED *reaches out, holds her.* DIDI *allows the contact, but skittishly.*)

FRED: Together, Didi. Together—I'll bet we'll have the temperature up to minus three hundred, or even two hundred-fifty. Hell, I'll bet minus two hundred-fifty will feel practically balmy to us after where we've been. We'll be sunbathing in it.

(FRED *starts to pull* DIDI *in the direction of the bedroom. She pulls away, and turns on him.*)

DIDI: You're still one of them!

FRED: What are you talking about?

DIDI: You're still one of them! You wouldn't be talking like that if you weren't.

FRED: No. We're the same—like and like, we're two of a kind. We're both worms. We're both vampires! That's the thing I understand now, Didi. I asked to understand just one thing, and now I do. I'm a wormy, vampirous nothing with an addiction to Coke and a life that matters less, in the scheme of things, than a former Beatles' ex-wife's leg wax—but—so what?

DIDI: Looks like I brought a live one home after all. Yes, that's some comfort. Cold comfort, as they say. *(She opens the door for him.)* Good-bye, Fred.

FRED: Good-bye? But, Didi—

DIDI: I can't do it to you, Fred. You've got so little left—it'd be wrong of me to feed on you.

FRED: Didi, haven't I proved that I'm just as cold and lost as you are?

DIDI: You still believe it's small, infinitesimal, but it's there. I can feel it—

FRED: No.

DIDI: I want to give in to the urge, but it would suck you dry. I can't do that to you, Fred.

FRED: All right. Maybe just a little. Maybe this much. *(He puts his fingers together in a pinch.)*

DIDI: Smaller.

FRED: Come on, Didi—

DIDI: Smaller.

FRED: *(Pinches even smaller)* Okay, this much, Didi, this much—

DIDI: Make it minute. Make it an infinitesimally small bit. SMALLER! Yes. That's it.

FRED: I know I've only got it left on the subatomic level, Didi! I admit that! I've got this much left. *(An impossibly small amount)* The same as you.
That's how we recognized each other, Didi. That's why we're here. It's small, infinitesimal. But it's there in both of us. It's still there.

DIDI: No, Fred, I don't have any left, I'm done, I'm tapped out, I'm—

(FRED takes DIDI's arm. But he is dragging her to the refrigerator, not the bedroom. He takes out the last Coke.)

FRED: First—take a swig.

(FRED *pops it open, hands it to* DIDI.)

DIDI: Coke gives me a headache. *(But she greedily gulps down as much as she can stand.)* All that sugar.

FRED: *(She hands it to him; he takes a big swig.)* Me too. So what? But at least now I know why it tastes like malted antifreeze.

(FRED *holds the can up to* DIDI's *lips, making her drink.)*

FRED: Come on, a little more, a little more. Now some for me.

(FRED *finishes it off, smashes the can in his hand, throws it away in a dramatic gesture over his shoulder, and drags* DIDI *toward the bedroom.)*

DIDI: Fred, please, I don't think we should jump into anything, sure, it looks solid to you now, but it could be a bottomless crevasse—you know how deceptive these Ice Ages can be—you think they're gone, then ten million years later—whoops—they're back—

(FRED *kisses* DIDI. *Pause)*

FRED: You're not a vampire, and you're not a worm. You've just been so cold for so long you've forgotten. But together—we'll remember.

DIDI: *(She rushes to the refrigerator.)* I need another coke— *(She opens the refrigerator. There's no more Coke.)* Oh. *(She closes the refrigerator door sadly.)* I guess that was the last one. Hey, let's go to the 7-11, we'll get another six-pack, we'll—

FRED: *(He shakes his head, and takes her hands.)* It's cold where we are, Didi, I'm not saying it's not. Nobody ever warned us it would get this cold. Somebody should have. Our mothers, maybe. Our fathers. But just because nobody told us is no excuse. It doesn't matter how cold it gets. We still have to believe.

That's what I understand. Yeah. So its okay now. I
understand.

(DIDI *lets* FRED *pull her to him, and she rests her head on his
chest.*)

DIDI: It turns out absolute zero's not so bad, after all.

FRED: Who knew?

DIDI: Not me.

FRED: Me either.

DIDI: It turns out the world at absolute zero—when
you get right down to it—the world at absolute zero
turns out not to be so absolute, at all.

(DIDI *and* FRED *kiss again.*)

(*Lights fade to blackout*)

END OF PLAY

A THING OF BEAUTY CAN
BE COPIED FOREVER

CHARACTERS & SETTING

BETTY, *a playwright. A little frazzled. Her plays are really funny.*

DAVE, *The God of Copy. The most redundant god in the world.*

A basement in a building where new work is developed. Other than stacks of old copies and files and janitor supplies, the only thing in the room is a huge, slightly ancient-mythic looking copy machine.

BETTY: *(To audience)* One day, I went down to the basement to make six copies of my new play. I was having a reading of it in twenty-nine minutes. On the outside, I looked perfectly calm, almost serene. Nothing showed above the water line, you know? But on the inside—I was exploding. I should have made those copies days ago. I should have made sure they were perfect, collated, each marked with the reader's name and the part they were playing. I should not have put myself at the mercy of a machine at the last minute, because we all know what happens when you do that. But I did it anyway. So on the outside—I looked serene. But on the inside I was screaming a gut wrenching soul eating mantra of copy need that sounded like this:

Six copies!

I have a to have six copies now now now now now!

Six copies!

Don't jam in the feed

Or get choked around the drum

Don't run out of toner don't let the contrast control go nuts and give me dirty grey pages where the words smear around like grave rubbings

Please let the collation work, don't screw it up, I can't stand it when that happens, I bet there isn't any three hole paper

THERE ISN'T ANY THREE HOLE PAPER I KNEW THERE WOULDN'T BE ANY THREE HOLE PAPER

I'll have to punch the goddam three holes myself, OH

GOD let there be enough toner let there be contrast and collation and clean clean copy god please.

DAVE: *(Appearing magically more or less from behind the copy machine with some paltry special effects)* Copy is both a noun and a verb, did you know that? So is reprint. So is mirror. So is clone.

BETTY: Who are you?

DAVE: Who am I? I AM DAVE, THE GOD OF COPY—the least original god in the universe. Cliché and Redundancy, and Redundancy and Cliché is my middle name. Who were you expecting? The Virgin Mary?

BETTY: Well, actually I was hoping you were the intern in charge of the copy machine.

DAVE: An intern? Oh, like an acolyte. How charming. God mistaken for mere mortal at his own temple. Now I suppose tradition demands I bend you over the altar and we make fuzzy grained images of a torrid sexual display?

BETTY: Sex wasn't exactly what I had in mind.

DAVE: Why not? All it is is reproduction.

BETTY: No sex. Copies are what I want. And I want them now.

DAVE: Well, of course you do.

BETTY: *(To audience)* And I did. That's the thing. I had to have those six copies the way Rapunzel's mother had to have that rampion.

DAVE: Hand over your originals.

(BETTY *does.* DAVE *looks at them, rifling through them.*)

BETTY: What is it?

DAVE: These aren't originals. They're already copies. Copies with staples torn out and dog-eared edges.

BETTY: I never had any trouble copying copies before.

DAVE: So? History does not always repeat itself, you know. Sometimes it just stutters.

BETTY: Look—I'll hand feed all the pages so they won't jam, okay. Will that make you happy?

DAVE: Happy? Happy? You know what would make me happy? CARBON PAPER! THAT would make me happy.

BETTY: But nobody uses carbon paper anymore—

DAVE: I KNOW THAT. Don't you think I know that? Oh for the days of carbon paper. With carbon paper you got a prayer a copy! You could get thousands of separate prayers from a single office—a couple hundred thousand from a city block each business day! Every time someone fed the sheets in between the roller they bowed their heads in prayer. Will the copy be clear enough clean enough strong enough? Should I use a new sheet of carbon paper or will this one be okay? Will it last another day? A prayer a page. That would make me happy. Not this—mass produced slap dash a hundred pages at a time urgent give it to me quickly, correctly clearly cleanly command passing as a prayer. Entitlement. That's what they call this. I should know, I was the first god to know about entitlement—except for the God of Entitlement, of course, who was entitled to know about it before me.

BETTY: Look—I'm sorry about your loss—but about my copies—

DAVE: A clear clean copy used to be a work of art! I should have nipped this technology craze in the bud with Guttenberg. Pre-Printing Press Europe—now those were the days!! Illuminated manuscripts—gold leafed, hand lettered, in poorly lit rooms, crammed

with hunchbacked monks, they prayed and prayed and
they copied maybe ten pages a day! And little Torah
scribes—before they can even THINK about copying
a word they have to obey six hundred and thirteen
commandments, sleep with their wives on Friday, and
if they make a mistake or run out of ink while copying
God's name they have to burn the whole thing and
start from the beginning—even if they're on the very
last page! Now that's the kind of copy we need! Copy
that costs! Copy that bleeds!

Now, people get copy like it was nothing. They never
pray. They curse, of course, at jams, at mis-feeds. But
pray?

BETTY: Look—tell you what—you just give me my
originals back and I'll go over to Kinkos up the street,
it's ten cents a page there, but I really do need the copy,
so—

DAVE: COPY IS CHEAP!! It's so cheap it's not worth
a single prayer. Yours was the first copy prayer I've
heard in a month.

BETTY: Ten cents a page is not cheap, Dave.

DAVE: Oh, really. Do you know how much it would
cost to make six copies of this little masterwork of
yours in, say, 57 B C? Adjusted to reflect the value of
the dollar today? Let me see…six copies, a hundred
and ten pages…so that's six hundred and sixty pieces
of papyrus…five slaves working twelve hours a day—
would make two sheets a day…that's room and board
for five slaves a year or so…then the scribe starts to
copy…his output averages one page a day—that's two
years work. We'll give the papyrus making slaves pay
comparable to a skilled technician—in the solid state
chip field—and the scribe—say, we'll compensate him
as if he were the nation's top brain surgeon. So. Seven

hundred and fifty thousand dollars. That's what your precious six copies should cost today.

BETTY: I don't carry that much money on me.

DAVE: I'll take a check.

BETTY: Look—I can't pay three quarters of a million for copy.

DAVE: Why not? Five minutes ago it was a matter of life and death. Five minutes ago, your need for copy was extreme.

BETTY: *(To audience)* He had me dead to rights on that one. Still, I stood firm. *(To DAVE)* Ten cents a copy—that's what I'm prepared to pay.

DAVE: Kinkos can give you six clear, clean copies for a few pennies—but can they make a deal to give you clear, clean copy for the rest of your life?

BETTY: What?

DAVE: Don't ask me to repeat myself, Betty. It isn't a pretty sight.

BETTY: *(To audience)* Now, a five year old child would have known better than to get sucked into a bargain with a minor deity in a dim basement. But the copy need was deep in me. I couldn't see the forest for the stacks of twenty pound three hole punch reams. *(To DAVE)* You can really fix it so I can get clear clean copy for the rest of my life?

DAVE: Of course. I am the God of Copy, aren't I?

BETTY: Will I have to go to a copy machine, or will the copies just…appear every time a new draft is complete?

DAVE: Sorry. Every copy machine or printer or earth is included in the deal, but you'll have to make a side deal with Domino, the God of Delivery for any kind of door to door thing.

BETTY: Oh.

DAVE: But when you do go get your copy, Betty—imagine—you'll never have to wait in line at Kinkos. Your printer will never jam, or mis-feed—you'll never get dirty copy, the machines will never run out of toner, there will always be abundant quantities of three hole paper, there will never be pages mysteriously missing, every script will be perfect, pristine, complete. And, as an unadvertised bonus—I am prepared to correct one spelling error per page.

BETTY: You can do that?

DAVE: Spelling's just copying on a conceptual level, after all. Well?

BETTY: Clear, clean, hassle free copy—for the rest of my life...I guess it's going to cost a little more than ten cents a page, right?

DAVE: Right. The price is—your sense of well being when you wake up in the black, small hours of the long desolate night.

BETTY: My sense of well being—

BETTY/DAVE: (Prompting her) When you/I awake up in the black small hours of the long, desolate night.

DAVE: Yes.

BETTY: I didn't know I had that.

DAVE: You will when it's gone. Don't play dumb with me, Betty. I am asking for your soul.

BETTY: You couldn't ask for something else?

DAVE: You haven't got much of anything else left. You're a playwright.

BETTY: Oh. Right.

DAVE: Well. What have you got to lose?

BETTY: My soul, apparently.

DAVE: Betty—you've given up everything else, right?
Fifteen point three years ago you said, and I quote,
"Just let me write! That's all I ask for! Let me write and
I don't care about fame, about money, about any of it!
JUST LET ME WRITE!"

BETTY: I don't think I said the word Fame, I mean it just
isn't my kind of word, it—

DAVE: But the gist Betty, the gist of it. Isn't that what
you said you'd sacrifice for your art? Didn't you offer
to give up everything other people wanted and got, if
only you could write?

BETTY: Well…yes. I never thought they were actually
going to take me up on it, though.

DAVE: You're writing, aren't you?

BETTY: Well, yes, but—

DAVE: Don't be so naïve, Betty. If you hadn't made
that deal you would have thrown in the towel in 2002,
gotten your Realtors license in 2006, lost it during the
crash in 2008, and been indicted for pyramid fraud
while selling NuSkin products in Encino last month.
Clean. Clear. Quick, eternal copy. Going twice. Going
twice. Going—

BETTY: I'll take it.

DAVE: Sold.

(DAVE *magically produces six copies of* BETTY'*s script, and
with a flourish, hands them to her. She looks at them, out of
habit, starts to page through the pages*)

No need to check, Betty.

BETTY: But I always go through each page to make
sure—

DAVE: It's perfect copy, Betty. From the hand of god.
What more assurance do you need?

(BETTY *sheepishly stops checking, hugs the copies to her chest.*)

DAVE: Well…this is it. Another repetitive, un-illuminating manuscript moment of want and diminished expectations in the double time of copy history—another meaningless rerun that changes nothing. While the great ditto master mandala of the human race spins on. *(He turns to go, then turns back.)* Oh, and by the way…

BETTY: *(Expectantly)* Yes?

DAVE: Your second act needs rewriting. *(He vanishes, with a half baked flourish.)*

BETTY: *(Bitterly)* Thanks. *(To audience)* So. That's how it happened. How I sold my soul for clear, clean, copy. Now some of you would say I should have held out for the God of Box Office. Or the God of Mainstage Regional Productions—or the God of Good Reviews—or any of the gods we all pray to, on a daily basis. But I say—sometimes you have to love the god you're with. And anyway—if I ever do run into one of the major theatre gods—you think I won't be able to make the same deal with them too? Of course I will. Selling your soul has gotten a lot of bad press over the centuries, but what's the transaction really about? It's about wanting something so deeply that it's worth your soul. And that can't be all bad. And so, in the theatre, you can sell your soul as many times as you have to. To every single one of the theatre gods there are. If the God of Writing a Play That Truly Means Something to the People Who Come and See It ever visits me and asks for my soul—and I pray, every day, that she does—we'll be good to go. Because no matter how many times you sell your soul—it's still there, to sell the next time. It makes a clear, clean copy of itself, somehow, in the moment you decide whatever you're

longing and striving for is worth everything you've
got.
A thing of beauty can be copied forever. That's the
thing I learned from my encounter with Dave, the God
of Copy. And I also got fabulous copy. Ask anybody.
They'll tell you. Betty's copy is perfect. Pristine.
Complete.

END OF PLAY

www.ingramcontent.com/pod-product-compliance
Lightning Source LLC
Chambersburg PA
CBHW052159090426
42741CB00010B/2331

* 9 7 8 0 8 8 1 4 5 5 5 0 2 *